1 9 9 1

Books and Chapbooks by A. Poulin, Jr.

POETRY

In Advent: Poems, 1972

Catawba: Omens, Prayers & Songs, 1977

The Widow's Taboo: Poems After the Catawba, 1977

The Nameless Garden, 1978

The Slaughter of Pigs, 1981

A Nest of Sonnets, 1986

A Momentary Order, 1987

Cave Dwellers, 1991

TRANSLATION

Duino Elegies and The Sonnets to Orpheus (Rainer Maria Rilke), 1977

Saltimbanques (French Prose Poems by Rainer Maria Rilke), 1978

The Roses &The Windows (French Sequences by Rainer Maria Rilke), 1979

Poems (French Poems by Anne Hébert), 1980

The Astonishment of Origins (French Sequences by Rainer Maria Rilke), 1982

Orchards (A Sequence of French Poems by Rainer Maria Rilke), 1982

The Migration of Powers (French Poems by Rainer Maria Rilke), 1984

The Complete French Poems of Rainer Maria Rilke, 1986

Anne Hébert: Selected Poems, 1987

ANTHOLOGIES

The American Folk Scene: Dimensions of the Folksong Revival.
Co-Editor with David A. DeTurk, 1967

Contemporary American Poetry. First Edition, 1971; Fifth Edition, 1991

A Ballet for the Ear: Interviews, Essays, and Reviews, by John Logan, 1983

CAVE DWELLERS

Poems by A. Poulin, Jr.

GRAYWOLF PRESS / ST. PAUL

Publication of this volume is made possible
by generous donations Graywolf Press receives
from corporations, foundations, and individuals,
including the National Endowment for the Arts,
the Minnesota State Arts Board, and
the McKnight Foundation. Graywolf Press is a
member organization of United Arts, Saint Paul.

Published by G R A Y W O L F   P R E S S
2402 University Avenue, Suite 203
Saint Paul, Minnesota 55114
All rights reserved.

Library of Congress Cataloging-in-Publication Data
Poulin, A.
Cave dwellers : poems / A. Poulin, Jr.
p.   cm.
I. Title.
PS3 5 6 6 . 0 7 8 C 3 3   1 9 9 1
8 1 1 '. 5 4 — d c   2 0   9 0 - 2 1 2 0 7
I S B N 1-55597-139-3

First printing 1991
9   8   7   6   5   4   3   2

ACKNOWLEDGMENTS

Grateful acknowledgment is made to the editors of journals in which some of the poems in this book (or earlier versions of them) were originally published:

The American Poetry Review: "Elegy," "River Snake" and "Salamander"; *The Atlantic Monthly:* "The Angels of the American Dream"; *Bits:* "Red Clock"; *Blackbird Circle:* "Oak-Dream"; *Boundary 2:* "The Angel of Oblivion," "The Angel of the Gate," "The Angel of Imagination" and "The Angels of Transmigration"; *Caim:* "The Angels of the Suburbs," "American Centaur," "Fists" and "Aubade"; *Chicago Review:* "The Angel of the Henhouse" and "Triptych: Self-Portrait"; *Choice:* "The Angels of Xanadu," "Angelic Orders" (Part II) and "Narcissus: Intaglio"; *College English:* "The Angels of New England" and "Landscape"; *Contemporary Literature in Translation:* "Birds," "Prayer to the Turtle," "Melon Patch" and "Widow's Taboo"; *Crazy Horse:* "Yearling"; *Esquire:* "The Angels of Quasars"; *The Iowa Review:* "Fireflies"; *The Kenyon Review* (First Series): "Angelic Orders" (Part I); *Memphis State Review:* "Siamese in Sunlight"; *Mid-American Review:* "The Forest Lawn Community Mausoleum"; *Mushroom:* "Song of the Sick"; *New Directions:* "Sea Monkeys," "Ground Zero," "The Angels of Youth," "The Angels of Love" and "The Elephant's Womb"; *The New England Review:* "The Voices"; *The North American Review:* "The Angel of Zealots"; *Outlaw:* "Juan's Song"; *Poetry Northwest:* "The Angels of the Underground" and "The Angels of Vietnam"; *Poetry Now:* "My Mailman," "The Scavenger of Albion," "Cartesian Char Woman" and "Moon-Rocks"; *Prairie Schooner:* "The Angels of Criticism" and "The Angels of Poetry"; *Quarterly West:* "The Killers"; *Rapport:* "Catoblepas: Anthony's Temptation" and "Lucifer Falling"; *Shenandoah:* "Bombardier" and "Flute Making"; *South Carolina Review:* "Shadows"; *Sou'Wester:* "Famine"; *Strivers' Row:* "The Moth"; *Tar River Poetry:* "Gross National Product," "Two Harvests," "Migrating Season," "The Wait" and "Fall Light"; *Transatlantic Review:* "Doppelganger"; *West Hills Review:* "The Angel of DNA"; *Williwaw:* "The Angels of Birth," "The Angels of Eternal Life," "The Angels of Film," "The Angels of the Jungle," "The Angels of Knowledge," "The Angel of Molecules" and "The Angel of the Wolf Pack."

"Cave Dwellers" was originally published by The Poetry Room of The Library of Congress (March 13, 1978) while Robert Hayden was Consultant in Poetry.

Some of the poems in this book (or earlier versions of them in different contexts) also were initially collected in some of my other books and chapbooks.

The inscription for Part I, "Angelic Orders: A Bestiary of Angels," is from "On Angels" by Donald Barthelme, collected in *City Life,* copyright © 1968 by Donald Barthelme, and reprinted with the permission of Wylie, Aitken & Stone, Inc.

The inscription for Part II, "The Elephant's Womb: A Bestiary of the Will," is from *The Book of Imaginary Beings,* copyright © 1969 by Jorge Luis Borges, and reprinted with the permission of E.P. Dutton & Co., Inc.

The inscription for the poem "Doppelganger" is the title of one of the original *Star Trek* episodes.

The inscription for and all italicized lines and stanzas in the poem "Letters from the Tower" are from a poem by Robin Morgan entitled "White Sound" (*Depth Perception,* Doubleday & Co., copyright © 1982 by Robin Morgan) which was unpublished at the time I read it and reprinted here with the permission of the author.

I am grateful to Dale Davis, Costas Evangelatos, Kimon Friar, Sam Hamill, William Heyen, Steven Huff, John Logan, Peter Makuck, Robert Phillips, Anthony Piccione, Tree Swenson, Scott Walker, and Michael Waters, as well as to my assistant, Michelle Simel, for their continuing friendship and encouragement.

To my wife, Basilike, my daughter, Daphne, and to Peter Hunzek, I am immeasurably grateful for their presence and humbled by their love.

—A.P., JR.

for

BASILIKE, MY WIFE

and for

DAPHNE, OUR DAUGHTER

CONTENTS

I. *Angelic Orders: A Bestiary of Angels*

ANGELIC ORDERS / 3

THE ANGELS OF THE AMERICAN DREAM / 7

THE ANGELS OF BIRTH / 9

THE ANGELS OF CRITICISM / 10

THE ANGEL OF DNA / 11

THE ANGELS OF ETERNAL LIFE / 13

THE ANGELS OF FILM / 14

THE ANGEL OF THE GATE / 15

THE ANGEL OF THE HENHOUSE / 16

THE ANGEL OF IMAGINATION / 18

THE ANGELS OF THE JUNGLE / 19

THE ANGELS OF KNOWLEDGE / 20

THE ANGELS OF LOVE / 21

THE ANGEL OF MOLECULES / 22

THE ANGELS OF NEW ENGLAND / 23

THE ANGEL OF OBLIVION / 24

THE ANGELS OF POETRY / 25

THE ANGELS OF QUASARS / 26

THE ANGELS OF RADIATORS / 27

THE ANGELS OF THE SUBURBS / 28

THE ANGELS OF TRANSMIGRATION / 29

THE ANGELS OF THE UNDERGROUND / 30

THE ANGELS OF VIETNAM / 31

THE ANGEL OF THE WOLF PACK / 32

THE ANGELS OF XANADU / 33

THE ANGELS OF YOUTH / 34

THE ANGEL OF ZEALOTS / 35

LUCIFER, FALLING / 37

II. The Elephant's Womb: A Bestiary of the Will

AMERICAN CENTAURS / 41

BOMBARDIER / 42

CATOBLEPAS: ANTHONY'S TEMPTATION / 43

DOPPLEGANGER / 44

THE ELEPHANT'S WOMB / 45

FISTS / 46

GROSS NATIONAL PRODUCT / 47

HYENA / 48

ICHTUS / 49

JUAN'S SONG / 50

THE KILLERS / 51

THE LION / 52

THE MOTH / 53

NARCISSUS: INTAGLIO / 54

OAK-DREAM / 56

THE PANTHER / 57

QUARRY: ELM / 58

RED CLOCK / 59

SEA MONKEYS / 60

TRIPTYCH: SELF-PORTRAIT / 61

THE UNDINES / 63

THE VOICES / 64

WREATH / 65

X-RAY: SELF-PORTRAIT IN FALL / 66

YEARLING / 67

GROUND ZERO / 68

III. Letters from the Tower / 71

IV. Cave Dwellers

FAMINE / 83

LANDSCAPE / 84

TESTAMENT / 86

TO: E P (K) / 87

SHIVA / 88

MY MAILMAN / 90

THE SCAVENGER OF ALBION / 92

FIREFLIES / 94

WILDEBEEST IN SUNLIGHT / 96

THE FOREST LAWN COMMUNITY MAUSOLEUM / 98

TWO HARVESTS / 100

OMENS, PRAYERS & SONGS:
POEMS AFTER THE CATAWBA / 101
Birds
Burning Sassafras
River Snake
Luck-Dreams
Salamander
Prayer to the Turtle
Melon Patch
Hungry Birds
Possum Hunting
Song of the Sick
Dancing Ghosts
Widow's Taboo

MIGRATING SEASON / 105

GEESE / 106

MOON-ROCKS / 108

FALL LIGHT / 110

CARTESIAN CHAR WOMAN / 111

FLUTE MAKING / 113

TOTEM / 115

AUBADE / 116

EASTER SUNDAY / 117

CAVE DWELLERS / 118

CAVE DWELLERS

Vous serez pour vous-mêmes, come la nature et l'histoire, un monstre.
—NIETZSCHE

* I *

ANGELIC
ORDERS

A Bestiary of Angels

The death of God left the angels in a strange position. They were over-
taken suddenly by a fundamental question. . . . How did they "look"
at the instant the question invaded them, flooding the angelic con-
sciousness, taking hold with terrifying force? The question was, "What
are angels?"

New to questioning, unaccustomed to terror, unskilled in aloneness,
the angels . . . fell into despair.

— DONALD BARTHELME

Angelic Orders

I've been seeing angels recently.
Green ones, mostly.
They look like trees.

Some are domestic: fruit trees,
maples, elms, and oaks. They run
after me. They whine when I ignore
them and walk by. They pelt me
with acorns, spit syrup at my head.
They throw tantrums and break birds.

Some are olive trees rooted
for centuries in the stony
landscape of my memory's holy land.
Others are ethereal:
willows rising by the river,
shimmering with ecstasy.

I don't know what to make of one
of them. It's in my bedroom
every night. A cyprus, it's
dark green, almost black.

It is tall, serene. Or it trembles,
gathering a storm above a field of red
and fierce, intolerable poppies.
It is glowing softly, moaning.
It is waiting   waiting

Clocks are angels, too:
their phosphorescent faces
glowing pale green through
the night, clucking minutes
one by one and filling up
my room with incandescent
feathers. And radiators,
as I've said before, are
angels. The refrigerator
is an angel: squat and square,
guarding meats and vegetables
and milk inside the steady
cold of its folded wings
where a light mysteriously burns.

The rocking chair's an Early
American Angel. Sometimes,
in the middle of the night,
I wake up and hear it
creaking softly, creaking
like the wrath of God or
the noise among dry bones
waxing louder and louder.

Flags are captured angels.
Flags are captured archangels
tearing their wing tips
on the wind and clawing
for escape. And blankets,
sent from such heights as
lovers come from, are angels.
Asleep, I am thin and white, stirring.

But doors are solid, flat
angels. They are always
there, pure as triangles,
faceless and essential,
locking me out of rivers,
barring me from fields,
from houses, and from mansions
I must enter   I must enter

III

But that is only half
of it. The fact is,
I don't only see

angels, I am one.
When I'm alone
at night, I draw all

the drapes, and in
that total darkness
I become an angel.

I stand stark still
and naked. I don't
stir until I feel

a fierce, unearthly
stirring in the pool
of my belly, the seed

of a thousand saviors
gathering like
a galaxy. My bones

are flutes for the word
of God, and sunlight
streams in my arteries.

At last I glow —
all white. I tremble.
My hair is the moon.

Wingless, unfeathered,
I am translucent.
I am fleshless. Pure.

I rise. I hover
above the city.
I visit virgins.

*

The Angels of the American Dream

Dazzling and tremendous, how quick the sun-rise would kill me
If I could not always send sun-rise out of me.
                                    —WALT WHITMAN

We are infested with light.
It gathers on the floor of the sea
that tides in the cave of our pelvis;
it sprouts on the limbs of our lungs,
branches over cliffs in our brain,
a bush burning law in a nation.

An organism from an alien world
rocketed down to test and possess
this planet, it feeds on the darkness
that breeds in the core of our cells,
on the pure filtered air in our blood.
Overnight millions of filaments

root and are thriving. By morning
our skin is transparent, our bones
are black, and we're radioactive,
barbarously bright. Ablaze
with amazement, we stay in our
bed all day, eclipsing the sun

in its orbit. Afraid we'll diffuse,
we don't move, not a muscle
or bone or an eye-beam. Still
by noon we can feel citizens
disintegrating on streets,
murdered by light. Seasons

accelerate. In the wink of an eye,
blossoms are apples that ripen

flames, and clusters of grapes
are coals. Buffalos burn to a crisp
on the spit of their bones. The sea pulls

to a dead stop. Whales rise like zeppelins.
By midnight the earth is pure mineral
ore, melting to white at its center.
Ravenous, we embark

*

The Angels of Birth

The sun explodes around my house,
blinding as the resurrection.
It is morning. Angels are swooping
purple shadows, shedding their clothes.
Oh, hundreds of naked angels in the naked
air! And Jesus is walking into the east,
the shape of an inviolate man on his back.

From the bedroom, down the stairs,
to the back porch, I stalk a trail
of blood: hands blooming on the walls,
fingerprints frying on the windowpanes.
These aren't my hands, my feet. I will
never find my way out of this labyrinth.

Angels have started attacking my walls,
battering my doors, clawing my windows.
And my name is falling from their mouths,
a skin for the stranger rising in my body.

*

The Angels of Criticism

They live
in ruins. Each
finger is a different
tool: a little hammer, chisel,
pick. Their thumbs are spades, eyes
the bristles of their souls. Their heads
sluice the darkest past for tiny skulls, for
relics, artifacts of any dried up god, and their
chests are the empty chambers they pillage. They decipher
the hearts of pebbles. They carve that secret on their wrists
and then they annihilate anyone who will not worship it or needs to.

*

The Angel of DNA

After a Photograph of Joe Brainard by Gerard Malanga

There is nothing behind you but the hint of energy's first spectrum: white to diaphanous gray. Your skull's a prism, the spectral angle jutting out your ear. And the last flagella's swimming out of sight.

So much of you is missing: your feet tangled in algae, the rippled bark of your calves and thighs, the immeasurable weight and ache of history ripening in your scrotum for the press, the gates of your hips soldered into the fate of male, even your torso, a riverbed without a trace of that one knot to betray your link with others of your kind, the chain that never can be broken. A fugitive from the improbable landscape memory obliterates, you are planted in this plot of time, trapped inside this frame of film like all of us, even if so much of you is missing.

You're the contradiction in our genes we would siphon out, but more elusive than deoxyribonucleic acid. In a glance you're the brink between the brute devouring the marrow to survive and the impossible fusion from father to lover, the pause between the grunt of stones and speech transfigured into song. Your mouth and eyes are the shift from senseless terror to the inscrutable smile of symphonies sculptured by saints. Your hair would turn us into shade, your eyes' brilliant holes of light dissolve us into stones. Afraid to look at you, we can't risk not to: our acid's essential contradiction.

And there is nothing between us, just your fingers curved into the first gesture of a tongue about to curl into a fist by instinct, shatter both of us out of this dimension. Still, I know you, stranger: my lost self betrayed by the mirrors of my eyes, eyelids of my words. I feel you writhing in the thinning space beneath my skin, contradicting who I am and what I do, hauling me beyond the memory of my own measured history, up the sands of a torrential river, back into a blinding spectrum.

Until then, except for our hands and tongues arched toward one another and the rays of our eyes refracted by the lens our breath's about to cloud, there is nothing between us.

*

The Angels of Eternal Life

If they remain alone, they never die.
Their unmatched molecules are perfect,
charged with energy distilled of
entropy. Forever radiant with that
one moment when they were utterly
happy and fulfilled light years before
their birth, their eyes are moons
staring at the sun, all day, all night.

But they have to know each other. So
they walk the streets, searching empty
eyes of other beautiful strangers,
desperate for one glimpse of such in-
human ecstasy. And when they find
each other, look, then stare with all
the fury of their awesome loneliness,
slowly they become transfigured into
lovers married years ago, fading and
defaced reflections of each other.

The Angels of Film

Eyes. Eyes. They are the eyes
that feed on children in the sun,
on brides, birds, grandmothers, stars.
They're always there, loaded revolvers
blinking too loudly at parties, shooting
at smiling faces with more vengeance
than crime or conscience. They capture
our gestures, helpless in their sight,
just to prove the past or present real.
We were children, once; beneath this
face there is another we have never
wanted. Our bodies just keep going,
developing reproductions of ourselves.
Our souls are prisoners of eyes forever.

The Angel of the Gate

After a Photograph of David Ignatow by Gerard Malanga

The gate is closed and guarded: veiled figures kneeling in their vigil, a kaddish of rock salt. A cross with broken arms leans like that obelisk near you cracking at the base. Lapped blank by rain, the sun's rough eager tongue, a slab slants to mark and close the angle's mouth. But yards of ground shrink back, sink to nourish the famished dead under the gentle weight of your eyes desperate to forgive and rescue them and us.

You aren't the center of this scene. You've been here all your life, one foot rooted in the ivy rooted in the eyes and throats, the pelvis of our common family. Off to one side and alone, your voice's bitter wisdom still charts avenues and roads, spans the gulf between worlds. Your words are clay bricks, markers for the murders of our love, monuments of what we are and do and leave behind.

If you turned to look this way right now, the earth would open like a broken eye, and the grass, the trees, our headstones, and our history would slip back into the gullet of that first and final film.

Instead, turn your back on us. Walk toward the world you've glimpsed behind the world. Release the giant in the dwarf. Let the leper bloom. Call the shrapnel of the factory worker back into a human shape. Charge the electric chair with grace. Give us the indestructible pulse of our own hearts again.

We'll follow. Speak: the gate will fly open.

*

The Angel of the Henhouse

You were bigger than me.
Your front teeth were separated
and you could whistle through them.
In the summer, when we drank
from the faucet near the barn,
you could squirt water
through your teeth, one long
stream, clear as a whistle.
You were Uncle Larry's pet.

You were stronger than me.
You could carry two baskets
full of eggs, one in each hand,
carry them downstairs even
on ice-covered steps in winter.
I slipped once, and the eggs,
a hundred melting suns,
crackled on the crusted ice.

You were older than me.
One day while Uncle Larry slept,
a self-made messenger from god
under a tree, you took me, your
captured cowboy, to your henhouse
tent where dust was piled high
as sunlight, and like a savage man

of medicine, with a feather's blade,
you opened up a wound in me to rid

my body of that arrow-head. Then
you taught me how to leave the echo
of your inhuman camouflage behind,
the figure of an angel in the dust.

The Angel of Imagination

I've been writing poems all night long.
Oh the lies and lovers I've invented,
the beautiful beasts I've become, more
awesome than those ageless archangels
in planetary jungles. And all night, in
the back corner of my eye, a face has
been staring at me, an enormous eye.

It has drilled a hole into my skull and
sees me through and through. It knows
the truth at the heart of lies, the lies
that are the strata of all art, and,
offering me a glimpse of the only world
I ever want to see, all night the echo
of a voice that is the spit and image
of my own has begged: *Dive into my iris.*

*

The Angels of the Jungle

The traffic of tourists has stopped.
The workers' trucks are still
silent. Above the humming of this
night's red heart, voices from lost
jungles are asking the same questions
over and over again: *Adam, where are
you? Where is your brother, Abel?*
Tonight I won't be the one to answer.

*

The Angels of Knowledge

Once they drank an indecipherable language
from a spring of wisdom at the center of
the jungle. They spoke with stars and were
murdered for what their tongues could never
translate into human thought or conquest,
greed, the power to rule space and atoms.

Generations of a forest rooted in this
earth's trembling core, their hearts
pumped a sap that was green with mystery.
Now each tiny leaf tongues its revenge:
no one can hear them and survive. You
fall into fits of knowledge, shuddering
a deadly wisdom. Mastered, your souls
fertilize their roots, their highest branch.

*

The Angels of Love

Disguised as shapes you love, lovers, friends,
and spouses, they are the princes of beasts.
You never learn to fear them or wage war
against them till they're just about to kill you.
Instead, you believe you are the creature
that they say you are. When your friend says
your right hand hurts him, cut it off.
Tear out your tongue: it can never please
your lover. Give your children your eyes.
Here, love, eat the heart of my last hope.

*

The Angel of Molecules

All day I've refused to be
everything I am: husband,
father, friend, and enemy
of any other living thing.
My will agreed and vanished
into space. But the slag
of cells, of history, my own
three decades of illusions
simply wouldn't melt. Then
tonight I began to feel all
my atoms rarefy. There!
I was that window... chair
... menorah... knife...
Oh angel of molecules, quick,
before I become this wor....

The Angels of New England

The rat's angelic chatter in the attic
and the furnace moaning its white fire
are familiar winter choruses in this
New Hampshire house shedding a century
of paint. And when the wind has died,
and if we hold our breath, from
the forest's heart of ice we can hear
the soft sweet vowels of our witches
singing as they burn.
                              Tonight the dark is
heavy on our lips, a yard of ground frozen
solid to its burning core. The white breath
of snow sprouts between the rocks; and chairs,
angel-headed tombstones glowing pale
as ice in moonlight, crouch. Under our
inherited handcarved headboard, waiting
for the slow loosening of our muscles'
rigor, we lie still as still-warm corpses
waiting for another song, a warmth, a sleep.

*

The Angel of Oblivion

The sun sucks mist out of your glass
skin. You shimmer, purer than dis-
tilled water. You're so luminous,
your ice-bones crack in calm frenzy.

Oh angel of oblivion, obliterate me
more. Wipe out my eyes. Spin my
spine with outrageous intent. Throw
me down in a fit of tongues I will
never remember. Burn another hand
full of cells. Make my future past.

*

The Angels of Poetry

Encapsulated in a ball of glass,
in that vacuum they are nothing,
invisible to the naked human eye.
Still, they think they are all those
images they feed on and believe
their voices magnify them into gods
prophets speak of, stones adore.

But no one's ever heard a thing
they've said. One was seen once:
a tiny thing, its head a speck
of mirror flashing a flea's tooth.
Still, they believe and sing at
such an inhuman pitch only dogs
and porpoises can hear, and
everything around them vanishes.

*

The Angels of Quasars

They're coming. Every night
I hear them coming: the whine
of their ships' incredible

annunciations far above
the cornfields at the city's
edge in the enormous dark

among the stars. Only dogs
and others like me hear them.
Their fantastic engines ring

grace in our bones. One day
they won't simply hover over
fields, visions for a few in-

somniacs. But they'll land.
They'll land swiftly, without
warning, right in the centers

of cities. As if promised
for centuries, they will dis-
embark, radiant, inhuman, and

glorious as gods stalking virgins.

*

The Angels of Radiators

Every night when my wife
and daughter are asleep
and I'm alone in this old house
lost in landscapes somewhere
between the points of stars,
my furnace fails like heaven.

The water that will turn
to steam and turn to heat
and rise as grace runs out.
In unlighted corners, angles
opening to blank space,
radiators, cold and white,
are silent and dead angels,
incarnate where they fell.

Every night, every winter,
I have to go down cellar,
turn the valve until the gauge
is full of water once again,
until the furnace starts
to rumble with its resurrection.
Then the house begins to move,
and through the winter night
that threatens us like Hell, by God,
the pure spirit of the fire roars
blue, veins ring, and radiators,
a whole chorus of Dominions, sing
and dance wild alleluias warm as spring.

*

The Angels of the Suburbs

Their faces are five fragile petals, delicate
unearthly velvet stitched by a single thought,
their very source and center. They're so thin,
they disappear in sunlight, evaporate in wind.
They stare at everyone with the serene surprise
the slaughter of sons couldn't alter. If you
stare back, you'll never be happy again or want
to. Their thought is relentless and implacable,
until they're blinded by night.

                                          Only then, if
you listen, if you listen with a mystic's ear
lost in ecstasy, or someone intent on learning
all the secrets of the earth, you might feel
their invisible fragrance singing by a window,
rising from the feet of cliffs, or falling off
rooftops. When you do, anchor yourself. Burn
blessed candles in both ears. Cut off your legs.

*

The Angels of Transmigration

They come in the middle of the night, in the dark.
Their bodies lost in shadows, their fur glows
with veins of gold and silver buried in them.
They speak to me with the sweet voices of lovers,
promising to tell me all the secrets of the dead,
show me the cities of ancient gods, future races,
and leave their precious antlers as gifts. But
they refuse to say what they'll ask for in return:
light, love, the mystery of children and of breath.

I won't comply. Bone and metal slash my sides.
My room trembles with the ecstatic cry of martyrs,
soldiers, my father's voice eaten by cancer's mechanisms.
This is the language of drills, the vowels of guns,
a tongue the dead teach to the living for the future.
Then in the morning's first, most fragile light,
brass hooves pound my chest; the smell of tombs
lost for centuries in the desert and the fine
metallic dust of holy hunters gathers in my mouth.

*

The Angels of the Underground

As if called by a voice
inhabiting the sun
crouching on a hilltop
and brooding over suburbs,
they come from behind
the gray, loose bark of
trees, beneath a stone.
They rise from the bone
and flesh of cattle
steaming in the fields
and alleys. They come
from the folds and seams
of our damp clothes, from
the roots of our hair.
They come from nowhere.

This morning the space
outside our window
filled with a universe
of seeds. Tonight swarms
of newborn larvae
gather into trembling
blue-green nebulae
inheriting our air.

And worms are stirring
under our soles,
rising to be crowned
princes of the earth.

*

The Angels of Vietnam

The morning liquefies.
I take one step, spring
up, and I am swimming
above branches of coral.
I breathe water. Delicate
fish dart through my eyes.
Gold and black, they are
angels nesting in my lungs.
And inside my skull they
sing shrill, barbarous
arias, chorals of kyries
at some inhuman pitch.
They shatter my bones.

Nothing weighs me down.
Men flicker like matches.
Whole cities are burning.
The Mississippi shines
with blood. I am rising
higher and higher. Whales
are winging me toward
planets pulsing like pearls,
space infested with sharks.

*

The Angel of the Wolf Pack

Animals stumble in pairs toward a tideless sea.
Blood floods the womb of all she-creatures.
Even the tiniest foetus stirring is aborted.

The angel's at my door, mouth frothing with moon.
His breath is warm against the transparent glass
of my skin. His paws stroke my hips and flanks.
His snarl unlocks a savage memory inside my cells.

I cling to the wilderness of his mane.
I give myself to him.
An emptiness in me I'd never known begins to fill
with his sweet foam. I will bear us a new breed.

*

The Angels of Xanadu

Springing from the dark
cool caverns in the earth,
fountains rising from
their own reflections,
willows on the muddy river-
bank are wholly still,
the palest green, waiting
to erupt, spit the lava
of their sap, shudder
glowing cinders, showers
that will singe our lips
with mystery and gentleness,
and solder them with grace
we will never understand.

The Angels of Youth

Wingless, the babies scratch
in the corner shadows, their skin
shredded into fur. They snap
at your ankles, their eyes fierce
as knotholes in the sunlight
burning the walls of old barns.
If you look into them, you can see
the horror of your most private
hope. You climb the attic stairs.

Filling the sudden explosion of
dark, the shapeless memory of un-
remembered guilt, a terrible angel.
He raises one calm wing up to a beam,
and with the other gently offers you the rope.

The Angel of Zealots

I can hear you pacing
up and down between
our beds every night.

Your soles are silent,
as if, every night, you,
like a mystic, suffer

levitation for our sakes
and souls, and, chaste,
your body is as light

as dust, as silent
as the dark you are.
Only your rosary clicks.

You finger your beads:
dried bones of foetuses
answer your prayers.

In this third storey
hall hung with dead
Christs, three times

removed from both
the city and the world
below, we lie in rows,

sleepless as saints.
A bloodless bat,
you are our guardian

angel rustling nearby,
Gabriel at the door
of Eden, sword in hand,

driving us back in
until we have no choice
but to re-invent our sin.

Lucifer, Falling

My right calf has ached all week.
I was afraid of varicose veins
and blood clots. Now the ache's
reached the tendons just above
my ankle. God! I can feel my
right foot hardening into horn.

∗ II ∗

THE ELEPHANT'S WOMB

A Bestiary of the Will

Plato . . . would tell us that the child had already seen the tiger in a primal world of archetypes, and that now on seeing the tiger he recognizes it. Schopenhauer (even more wondrously) would tell us that the child looks at the tigers without fear because he is aware that he is the tigers and the tigers are him or, more accurately, that he and the tigers are both forms of that single essence, the Will.

—BORGES

It seems as if heaven had sent its insane angels into our world as to an asylum, and here they will break out in their native music and utter at intervals the words they have heard in heaven; then the mad fit returns and they mope and wallow like dogs.

—RALPH WALDO EMERSON

American Centaurs

After Lucretius and Historical Accounts

Surely the secret hand of God was in this.
It terrified the red men. They dropped
their weapons, and their cries streaked
the air with blood. Only some unthink-
able evil spirit could conjure such an
enemy. Neither man nor beast, it divided
to the arrow: the figure of the human fell
to the ground, and the horse galloped on
across the burning prairie into the sun.

That's how we inherited the earth. Now
our backs and flanks die fifty years too
soon. Staked on the mounds of our own
ashes, our heads turn toward the totem and
its eye slices supplication from our tongues.

*

Bombardier

I am fallling.
Inside my dead
mother, I am
falling through light
years of dark.

Rapids chew roots,
the bark of trees,
shattering boulders
with serrated foam —
ice flashing in this
summer moonlight.

From the lair
of my father's ribs
on the desert's river
bed my bones are born.

Catoblepas: Anthony's Temptation

I've looked at nothing but the ground or floor for weeks.
Filled with the thoughts of angels, calculations
of Kabbalists, my skull's become too heavy to hold up,
my neck the warm and stretched intestine of a buffalo.
Now my eyes are tracing paths of burnt grass where I walk.
Ants fizz into ashes. No one's looked at me for weeks,
as if afraid to die. Anthony, I'm afraid that if I
lifted my red and swollen lids, my eyes would kill
my daughter and my wife. My mirror would murder me.
Close your eyes, dear friend. Place your fingers on
each side of this enormous head. And with your thumbs,
with all the love you ever felt for me, crush my eyes back
into the mystery of this new power, or, look at me, *look at me*.

*

Doppelganger

But What of Lazarus?

Somehow he learned to break the barrier
of cosmic laws preventing our collision.
We watch each other in the mirror.
My right hand's his left fist, my thumb
on the opposite end of his hand. Right
now he's writing all of this backwards,
contradicting everything I think. He murders
when I make, my love's his hate, my prayer
his most precious blasphemy. We know:
if we should meet, the reflection of our eyes
would obliterate the galaxies inside of them.
This is my choice and his: to annihilate
counterbalanced histories with a final kiss,
or leap into that tunnel between his universe
and mine, and there, timeless, where law,
and blood and our own brotherhood will end,
forever wrestle one another for our brothers' sake.

The Elephant's Womb

A school of yellow and bright orange fish
swims above your bed. I wake up on land,
remembering and afraid, gasping for breath.
Your pink pig stands on its hind legs,
begging for pennies that shorten his life.
Monkeys swing from the wood of their elbows,
the knots of their eyes burning into mine.
The square elephant's head you made and were
one day has taken your room for its body.
Her eyes shining from another world fill up
with darkness, and I walk out of her side,
anxious to see you, anxious to see you are
still my daughter. Tonight, before you fall
asleep, or some other when you wake, screaming,
I'll tell you how we all must move from one
kingdom of beasts to another, and another,
how each is more treacherous than the last,
and what we have to strangle to survive.

Fists

Curled up in my lap
they are delicate nests
guarding blue-white eggs.

They're tiny hairless
cubs sleeping in the sun,
their pulse still harmless.

Flowers on film, they are
veined magnolias opening
in slow & perfect unison.

They are humming white
wings spinning a cocoon
for a rising sun or war.

*

Gross National Product

These trees tremble with a precious
ecstasy rising from their secret roots
and mines. This morning every vein
is throbbing, each bright leaf shines:
tongues that promise the ecstatic power
to carry us, our things, belongings,
our history away from all this business
of buying faces, selling eyes, trading
our souls and seeds in the open market
to survive. But they fall: a gaggle
of old lusts that fed too long on gold-
leafed heavens too extravagant to support
the bulk of the smallest human need.

*

Hyena

I've had to pillage sepulchres,
then chew up graves to feed our
insatiable hunger for emblems
of what we just might be. So far
we've survived: the dead flow in
our veins, water their immortal
hair sprouting just above our
genitals, blooming out our skulls,
souls sucked up by cosmic winds.

But those burying grounds grow
emptier by the minute. History's
interstices, toothless graves
laugh at the famine gnawing its
ravenous space inside of us and cave
in like mouths of ancient mothers.

Soon it will be just you and me.
Neither male nor female, I don't
have the luxury of preferences.
Hyena, I've devoured my own
vocal cords. Now listen: in this
space you are talking to yourself.

Ichtus

In the absolute darkness and silence
at the heart of night, I've knelt to you.
Like a pope, I've kissed the ground and dust,
stretched my arms out into the shape of
that relentless shadow erected in my memory
and nightmares. But you won't come down
or lift me up. Content to lord it over
me, a Byzantine king with brass for blood,
Christ, you're still an impossible bastard.
Blood, bread and fish of my deserted past,
in this jungle, see if you can save yourself.

Juan's Song

Drunk, I slept in my clothes.
All night my body was a barnyard
humming toward dawn. Dawn.
My hand, a kitten, uncurled in
the sun, my face a pink piglet's,
my toes, chicks scratching in the grass.

Purple necked, plumed gold and red
in the blazing sun, perched
on the fence of my open zipper,
my cock crowed and crowed and crowed.

*

The Killers

The hunter's back.
Trembling, his poised
scarred body's naked,
breathless in the breath-
less grass. Chained
to his wrist, my dog's
wild with his smell.
Glowing in moonlight,
he is harmless, mild.

I start to move. He
wills my every step.
When my breath begins
to tighten every muscle
to its highest pitch,
pry my mouth open with
a song no man has heard,
I leap into the center
of his eye, hear his bow
sigh and sigh, and feel
his bright burning arrow
entering the tender patch
of hair at the center
of my falling back.

He lifts me in his arms.
A small brown circle
starts to grow between
his pure white shoulders.
We kiss the throb
in one another's necks
and we forgive each other.

*

The Lion

Inside my mother's womb, I died
the day that I was born. Three days
later, my father came. Breathing
on my face, he scraped my mouth
open with his tongue, and my heart
leapt and yelped and roared its pulse.

I've survived the scorpions, the snakes,
the hunters' poisoned meats. I've taken
the monkey-based medicine prescribed
in all the books, and destroyed each
of my enemies with the brute force
of my own voice. And I have ruled.

Faster and stronger now, the earth
contracts each day. It's time for me
to die again. My cubs can't father me.

Guardian of kings' tombs, my father,
ruler of realms I'll never know, roar
and crack the granite of your mouth.
Tongue me another and another kingdom.

*

The Moth

In summer here the moths are big as birds.
No one dares go out at night. They used to
stampede cattle, once; now, late at night, they
dive at the last window lit with the frenzy
of light. Children think they feed on them.
Wanting to warn me, my neighbors say: Out there,
in the center of the dead grove of pines, silent
as a cocoon, one of them's bigger than a man.
He's the father of them all, a kind of Lord & God.

And I've waited for him all summer long.
I've stayed awake until dawn looking for him.
One night his eyes will burn, a fallen angel
at my window. His bright wings will tremble
with the promise of another ecstasy and peace.
The glass will melt. He'll hover vertically,
as if forever. But finally, with his thin lips
against my throat, he'll wrap me in the cool
darkness of his wings, space will disappear,
and I will rise again in that white silence
my brothers and neighbors have always feared.

*

Narcissus: Intaglio

He's lain in that same place so deeply
and so long, neither tide nor tourists

have erased the matrix of his body
pressed into the beach's brilliant sand,

the persistent echo of the lover
of an angel carved in snow. Inside this

dome of pure detachment from any human
presence but his own, all is ritual:

the slow ceremonial ballet
he dances to undress; the long liturgy

of lotions and of lubricants to screen
out any harmful ultra-violet ray; and

the astral mathematics he's devised
to calculate exactly the direction

and the angle that his body must assume
to burnish and to glow a deeper, a more

precious bronze. For hours he becomes this
blazing sun-dial's own incarnate shadow,

rotating at the center of attention,
the axis of our common day-to-day

anxiety: this young man's body is
quite simply just too perfect, just

too beautiful, intolerable, and dangerous.
If we stared into such beauty long enough,

we'd be effaced by our own humanity.
Wrapped in his cast of sheer oblivion,

he falls asleep and dreams his image
rising slowly from its intricate

intaglio etched across the beach's face,
a lover hovering in pleasure over him;

it is so stunning that it starts to fuse
the sand into a host of eager mirrors

out of which it rises, multiplied, again
and pollenates a galaxy of radiating

memories until the dream and dreamer are
one more possibility of beauty that has

vanished like an echo, here, in the ice-blue
absence of my eyes, the black behind my lid.

Oak-Dream

The oaks are bare
as osier baskets,
willows stiff, the
glowing skeletons
of ancestors' hair.
The stained gauze
of dogwood petals
is incinerated
and bare timbers
are sterilized
for cross-beams.

In my dreams, red
leaves are anon-
ymous mouths of all
friends and lovers
I have killed; they
bloom in revenge,
come back to devour
the first shoots
of gentleness and
charity sprouting
from my limbs in
years, ravenous
to live forever.

The Panther

I am alive and fully formed
inside my mother's womb.

For months her breath was mine.
She fed me with her blood's cells.

Now it's time for me to earn
the air I breathe, for my own

blood to carry me and to survive
any other creature who would

feed on me. I've started to claw
and chew. I am giving myself birth.

Quarry: Elm

Start with the limbs.
Saw off the bright, tender
ones rooted in the sun.

Let them tumble, wings
from an unearthly trunk.

The sun will moan
and leave a bright blue
wound, a scar of light.

And then the trunk.
Slice it down. Huge slabs.
Down until your saw is

burning, rings and rings
of imperceptible secrets,
amulets of generations
decoded, all defenses lost.

Leave the heart for those
who come hooded and armed
with syringes and serum,
mysterious as lovers.

Rooted in the soil of our
daily lives for centuries,
a shield against excessive,
unrelenting light and hope,
the gorgeous beast is dead.

*

Red Clock

I can hear it hum in silence.
Someone nailed his heart up on my wall,
ran out, and left me with his life.

Sea Monkeys

Fertilized by water, each pebble grows
its own arms and legs, a head, and bright
infinitesimal genitals that are sterile.
They tumble in the jungle of artificial
grass and dream of their children chattering
in the palms. One morning, all my fathers
and brothers have risen into the air.

Triptych: Self-Portrait

We've been below
the zero point
for days, locked
in the massive
cold front above
Kansas. Mornings
are blunt ice.
We suck our words,
and, fired glass,
our passions crack.
At noon the seas
at our sides
are bubbling hot
springs, oases.

This is my house.
I like it cold.
Tonight I sit
in the alcove,
do what I love
to do: listen
to the furnace
fail like heaven.
Radiators,
coiled and hollow,
hiss, a pack
of earnest priests.

In the mirrors
of my windows

leaded with ice,
I see three
treacherous
reflections
of myself.

*

The Undines

They spawned us
in our fathers' first wet dreams,
then outlived them and the memory
of pleasure thwarted by the threat
of sons. Now they surface to that
brim of our own loneliness as sons:
strangers cracking the porcelain
of our teeth with the unsatisfied
hope for a feeling we'd die for.

Water breaks. Words dissolve
in the solution of their dreams.
Mother! Naked, her shoulders cold
and green as kelp, she swims toward me.
The hair on her body and head,
hair that divided for my head, shining
iridescent scales in the watery blue.

Her mouth hunts mine, open, singing
of another and more lasting life.
The moon rocks us on a bed of sand.
Hair divides again, the sea muscadines,
and I slip into that deeper, final sleep
no man ever returns from, or wants to.

*

The Voices

The echoes of the past still lie
muffled by the wool's blue moss.

———

I slice the envelope's white lips
and they exhale the dust of ink:
survival's ancient alphabet flies
off into the gullet of the wind.

———

Plugged by solid plastic nipples,
the telephone sleeps in its cradle.
Minutes grow old by the minute,
each word jammed at the root.

———

Every poem in the book is blank.
Space to sleep in. Pages tear
and drown in the canal. I strip
off each milligram of sound I can.

———

The earth's a plaster on the moon's
shrill O. Beaks of stars ground
out. Every sheet swallows my words,
my cells devour their own hieroglyphs.

———

In the total silences of ruling
planets, I listen to the echoes
of beasts breathing in stones, in me.

*

Wreath

Curled up on your bed,
I am a wreath on our grave
working my way down.

X-Ray: Self-Portrait in Fall

Fall. Fields and forests
tremble with the blasts
of shot guns. The orange
ghosts of hunters burn
new trails through morning
mist. At noon, high above
the bay, Canadian geese
soar, precise, victorious.

The time has come.
I strip down to my own
white waist, and, stalking
hunters, roam the fields.

Inside my ribs, iridescent
as a cock pheasant,
my father's cancer flutters.

Yearling

I've stopped holding on.
Weeks ago I gave up
rescue, ghost and gravel.

My fingers are soldered
to rock, each bone taken
root, a hundred veins

of ore in an unfathom-
able mine. I am growing
out of the face of this rock.

Generals, sailors,
even presidents know
the grace of earth eating

skulls. I am praying wild
birds to sacrifice my wrists.
My feet have begun their ascension.

*

Ground Zero

At the vanishing point of the mirror's depth
of field, there's a shining, shifting fish.
In the bright sun or dark of sleep, it swims
in the blue of my cornea. Sometimes a tiger,
its color no color, it comes brightly ringed
with the clatter of weapons. This fish is
the first to come back from the improbable
land of mirrors. Prisoners of lead, condemned
to be repetitions of our dreams and acts,
they're beginning to stir now, to contradict
the angle of my finger, color of a scar.
Tusks defy teeth. Hooves trample my hair.
Tonight the sea is churning with the cries
of all its secret creatures, and the vague,
distant, but familiar outline of a man walks
toward the center of my eye. Free again,
they're coming back. Tomorrow morning I
will point a revolver at my face, and, knowing
who will win, one reflection will kiss and kill
the other in order to survive itself and me.

*

✻ III ✻

LETTERS FROM THE TOWER

It is not right for mourning to enter a home of poetry.

—SAPPHO

Letters from the Tower

(YADDO)

I

Every morning for the last two weeks, with nothing
    but blank sheets of paper and some sharpened pencils
        – tools of the only trade I know – I've climbed

the narrow tower stairs into this high ceilinged
    cell with its walls painted a pale ivory, sparsely
        furnished with a logic not my own: a chaise lounge

and a cot, a *prie dieu* leaning toward the bust
    of a sinister and adolescent saint near a picture-
        window overlooking distant mountains stretching out

beyond a vast expanse of swards sloping toward
    formal gardens of rare roses where granite statues
        of imported Grecian women, hoisting urns of what

must be ointments of crushed petals and exotic
    spices on their shoulders, keep a mute, immobile
        vigil near the flashing splash of man-made waterfalls.

Gazing down on such preternatural splendor,
    I could be a banished prince, the true successor
        to the throne, condemned here by my bastard brother,

His Majesty the King, to contemplate my fate,
    renounce all worldly goods, the glories of the coil,
        prepare my common soul for its imminent decapitation.

In this excess of white hush, I might be an Abbess
        come to meditate on Mary's sorrowful mysteries,
                my old and heavy body hovering about the room

in an anticipation of a modified assumption. . . . Shit,
        what's a peasant farmer's son doing here in this
                anachronistic fantasy of a decadent Victorian

who soothed her nerves, assuaged her pain by soaking
        her left hand in a basin full of warm opals while
                her della Robian dentist filled her mouth with gold?

I haven't come here every day to participate
        in anybody's history but my own. My memory
                is my only prison, premise, and assumption,

towering above the rubble of a life I worked
        and plotted to erect, then willfully demolished.
                My friend, like you, I've come here to survive myself.

                        Forgive me for not having heard
                        what your silence was saying more clearly;
                        I was busy calling you deaf.

                                II

                                I dream I can no longer

                tell the screams of a human from those of a jay:
                streetcurses, brakesqueal, sirens,
                the whining of a child, the sobs of a hostile lover,
                dreams of real wilderness, all muffled. . . .

But Christ, who *can* survive in such rarefied sur-
        rounds? The brilliant jams and marmalades shimmering
                in silver bowls beside the ringing crystal Waterfords;

morning eggs floating in a halo of fresh butter
      gleaming on the Limoges china as translucent
            as the wrists of wealthy dowagers in sunlight;

the literary pleasantries of the languid
      cocktail hour; the intimate exchange of gossip
            and of intimate neuroses; the orchestrated dinner

bells; the recitals in the private chapel
      after dinner; applause polite as murmured litanies;
            the whisper of long skirts across the parquet floors;

the slow, restrained, soft clicks of brass latches, locks and bolts.
      After all this luxury of manifest civility,
            when we are left with nothing but relentless

echoes in our chests, the utter destitution
      in our souls, the brutal silence of a night
            that may not end, of a morning that will surely

dawn too soon, my friend, will we comrades in art
      also spend this night contemplating the revolver's open
            mouth, the mantra pulsing from a stolen carving knife,

the lilting hum of phenobarbital and gin?
      And when dawn breaks, at last, will we awaken
            to discover that tableau and frieze – the massacre

of lovers, spouses, children that we planned
      and executed – intricately etched
            on the inside of our corneas?

                        I dream I am a siren singing underwater,

                        having lured myself to death.

What we deny, denies us.
What we make live in art denies us
if the blood spilled to it is anyone's
but our own. All else is white sound. . . .

With my lunch pail in one hand, papers in
    the other, I climb those stairs again, a faithful
        factory hand off to another day of honest work.

I could become accustomed to this way
    of life. While sunlight settles in the paint,
        I review the products of my last two shifts:

White sound.
    Calculated to drown out the more
        human noises of the heart, the howling

of the beast that crouches in the darkness
    of the brain. In self disgust I turn to
        the work of a revolutionary city woman.

                How dare we call the scream of a jay
                its natural sound simply because

White sound.
    The static of half-truths that would erase
        the cries of more than half the human race

                we've never heard it sing?

and in the black light of day come crashing
    down in its maker's complicated heart
        under the weight of history, day-to-day

Things happen

in translation.

reality, a chorus of mythology.
     Listen, I'm a millhand's and a farmer's
         son. I know the smell of blood spilled by

my own hand, in this life and that other.
     The whine of a hundred looms all in one
         room, the grunting howl of pigs that are being

led to slaughter, the grunt men make
     as they break, alone or with an other –
         all echo in my tonsured head, in each

cell of this body I have worked so hard
     to make delicate, refined, to generate its own
         white sound.

The death toll

mounts in Florida, where I was born –
black bodies falling like needles

Listen, who said these cultivated flower
     gardens, these rustic neo-classic paths
         among the pines, these forsythias

from a white pine tree. A volcano erupts.
Nothing so pacified, inert, or tame

masquerading as the burning bush
     on Sinai aren't the jungle they have
         always been? Who said the death toll would be

it can be trusted beyond a certain solstice
of gratuitous pain; the well-meant joke
                    of sex or race

higher in a southern city than in
        these northern hills? Who believes the blood
                of Cain flows less in the veins of artists

            the teller can afford to not hear clearly,
            all honorable men counting on laughter

than in us common laborers', regardless
        of their color, sex? And when Sappho chiseled
                her commandment forbidding mourning in

                to drown out the rude Polack strains
                of a Chopin étude. If a woman paces

a home of poetry, who said that in
        her other hand she wasn't holding
                the bloody disembodied head of Orpheus?

                in her room, black fists clenched white
                with anger; if a woman works in her cabin

White sound.
        Every woman's death diminishes you
                and me more, every man's. And still, and still,

                defying terror to understand another
                woman on her page; if a woman stalks

we and our art live by the death of others;
        and the blood that's spilled to it, the blood
                that steams in slaughter houses, battlefields,

herself on canvas; if a woman
builds herself a jade burial armor;

in the endless privacy of bath tubs is
      anybody's but our own. Listen,
            the crow and cardinal caw and sing

            if a woman walks in the woods and walks
            and walks and grinds her white forehead

to one another. The wild rabbit devours
      the forsythia. Your pet cat offers you
            the mangled, almost bloodless corpse

            against indifferent moss and weeps
            and rages at such weeping, what does it mean?

of the robin that's been hatching her blue
      eggs outside my study window –
            a humble homage to the hand that

            If a woman falls in the forest and
            no one hears, is there sound?

feeds her in the house of poetry where
      she was abandoned by another poet.
            Next door, a woman and a man are making

            If a man falls in the forest and
            no one hears . . .

love. In our respective cells,
      you and I are making poems about
            men and women making love and war.

Things happen

in translation.

White sound.

IV

There is a poem missing here
like the deliberate flaw the Navaho weaver
leaves in her blanket – to let the soul out.
That poem would be a luxury, a passion;
it could afford trust, it could have something
to do with love. . . .

I've been thinking about men all day, the sound they make when
there's no one around to hear them weaving sounds around a
flaw for their heart's own slow release.

This is the sound the new-born man-child makes as his foreskin is
sliced off for sanitary purposes that will not save his body or his
soul.

This is the sound the adolescent boy makes in his dreams as the
stranger with his father's voice laughs at that useless labia
wrapped around his thing, then hacks it off with his hunting
knife.

This is the sound that young men make when they sit together
drinking, talking on a porch in Saratoga Springs in a loneliness
that will never be consoled, and suddenly their words stiffen
their own tongues like violent strangers' cocks inside their
mouths.

This is the sound men make when the silence at the sight of a sud-
den tenderness in them shrivels up their eyes like testicles unex-
pectedly immersed in the cold blue of the Atlantic.

This is the sound men make when the seeds of some unspeakable love in them die in the pit of their own hands and suddenly burst into flames like sons.

This is the sound men make as they fall into pools of sunlight on the forest floor beneath the weight and worry of the unsung music in the story of Ulysses and Penelope.

This is the sound of one old man, drunk on brandy, as he tap-dances his Step-'n-Fetch routine alone in the moonlight when there's no one near to comfort him at dawn.

This is the sound men make as they vanish in the canvas that they thought they'd filled with their own lives.

This is the sound of men shattering in an intolerable symphony of muscle.

This is the sound men make when, because of mindless pleasantries of sex or race, their white fists pound brick walls until they're blue, then black, then bloody as a buck nigger's on the rack.

This is the sound of young men in a hundred foreign fields as they collapse beneath the kiss of their stranger brothers' bullets.

This is the sound of men in cubicles and cells, in jails, monasteries, submarines, as they invent themselves, trace the contours of their bodies with a creator's care, fill each other with the tender hum and power of their very lives, then, like ancient women, lie there as their souls escape through the flaws of their own hearts — with passion, trust, perhaps something to do with love.

This is the sound a boy makes as he's raped by his mother's or his father's lover.

This is the sound men make in their terrifying love of daughters who can never be protected from the sound men make.

This is the sound men make in the threadless maze of their love of women and of one another.

This is the sound of one man, forever in a forest of white sound, falling.

* IV *

CAVE
DWELLERS

Nos quidquid illud significat faciamus
et quam sit verum non laboremus.

—ST. AUGUSTINE

Famine

The cry of frogs rings the island, rings.
Bullets ricocheting off raw steel. Spring.
Tonight the full moon rises pure, precise,
and deadly cold. Everything will freeze.

Trees petrify, their first and fragile
leaves the clatter of slate chips. In
the garden, sharp white shoots are glowing
bones of young men rising in revenge.

Buds and bushes fall and shatter, empty
eggs and skulls of a generation turned
to salt. Our eyes turn and, marble, shine.
Our hands and feet root into veins of lead.

Our mouths already fill with sand.
And beyond the moonlight, in the dark dawn
will never break, we can hear the long and
eager moan of boulders as they mate and spawn.

*

Landscape

We are gargantuan. The Old Man
of the Mountain and his rock-face
wife. Between us, under our eyes
steady as granite, the landscape
is deserted, a desert of wood grain
rippling like dunes to our breath.

On a plateau smooth as ceramic,
shadows of silos salt and pepper
the matchbox cottages, their
roofs bearing orange and purple
suns ceaselessly burning night
and day. Any day now the tinder
will ignite, raze this development
fabricated overnight, unpeopled.

Beneath a tree whose branches
are a tight and yellow rose-
bud, the dead are only half
buried. Skin paper thin,
bones glowing, they stir
as if digging their own way
in or out of this unholy ground.

Last night we were a mountain,
unscaled. Our love was Himalayan.
We must have slept an epoch.
Overnight a glacier cut across

a continent and split us into
cliffs confronting one another:
two prehistoric creatures
about to battle for the same
empty village for our breakfast.

Testament

And now our bedroom's sealed,
the tomb of Pharaoh
stirring with huge spiders,

reincarnations of ourselves.
Your kiss devours me.
Our bed is an anthill.

With every cave and crevice
of our bodies full of honey,
trembling liquid gold, our

words, the teeth of memory,
begin their work. But our
bones are secret passage-

ways winding down to the center
of the earth where, leaping
up like lava, mysteries

are still unearthed, where love,
an offering left by the living
for the dead, can crystallize.

And there, love, among un-
discovered kings, we will not die.

*

To: E P (K)

In Memoriam

Like dust on table corners
left by Martha's old black hand,
you linger, unseen,
on the edges of my brain.
But when the light is right,
slanting at oppressive angles,
and disturbs the silent shadows
in my room and skull,
I see you, and I'm embarassed.
I make excuses to my friends:
"Forgetfulness is hard
to come by these days."
And with an unobtrusive
sweep of my own hand,
I brush your name aside
or cover up my memory
with some small book.

Shiva

My daughter draws a picture of me
and leaves it on the kitchen table.
It is morning, and I'm Shiva! My
body's purest pearl, my throat an
azure only beasts and angels see.
My gold trident flashes so, Louis
Quatorze would court me like a pope.
And, oh, my eyes are Hope Diamonds
in triplicate! I want to gallop around
town and up the mountain on my white
bull shouting: *The enemy will never*
come! We don't have to murder one
another! I want to be the world's
most beautiful penis dancing in
the streets, caressing eight or ten
people at once. I love to be adored.

Happy to be Shiva drinking coffee,
that my daughter loves me so and
worships me because I gave her life,
I want to give her still another one.
So, I look at my portrait once again.

I am naked! Around my neck, neck-
laces of skulls, hundreds of skulls,
her face waxed across each one.
Those are demons that were hoards
of lovers. At the center of each

eye, an insatiable hole in space.
My arms and penis, boa constrictors.

Oh my daughter, only five years old,
you already know that any god or father
can obliterate whatever he can make.

My Mailman

Every day I wait for him to come
driving on the wrong side of his
tiny red, white and blue truck,
park it right in front of my house.
I watch him hang his pouch around
his neck, a brown leather uterus
bulging with flat, rectangle eggs,
secrets my anonymous angel in gray
uniform hardly ever gets to know.

Then I wish I had the ancient right
to kill this messenger, enjoy him
dying in slow torture or wipe him
out as fast as he is ever nameless.
He brings me only *Vogue* and *Life*,
The Penny Saver, bills and letters
from old friends I've read before.
Oh, sometimes he brings money, books,
a word or phrase that comforts some.

But he's the messenger. He should
know how long I've waited, and for
so much more.
                    I am waiting for
my daughter's trembling hand, my
wife's tongue, my father telling
me he loves me in his own words
lost years ago and covered with
postmarks of places I've never heard
of or want to. I am waiting for
more time, more time, a doctor's
bill of health and a prescription

for muscle my flabby spirit never
had, for an absolute absolution.

I am waiting for that burning white
letter with no stamp, no return
address, no postmark, no more than
my name scratched in my own blood
and saying no more than *"Come!"*

The Scavenger of Albion

The teabag's wilted on the table.
She heats the tea until it's tepid
just enough to burn her lips and
stomach. She sips until it's cold,
until sunlight cracks the film of soot
on windows, raises dust on floors.
These days it takes so little less.

It's Monday. In the new cedar litter
baskets clamped to the corner lightposts
there'll be almost half a cord of *New
York Times* to roll into tight logs.
Bottles to sell. Near bars, glasses
and maybe a wool sweater or a shoe.
Pennies in churchyards and gutters.
The telephone booths small mines.

A ray touches her temple: her eyes
sleep again for a minute that could
last forever. She dreams the dream
she's dreamt so often and so long,
she's forgotten when it all began
and knows each small detail by heart.

There are phone booths on every corner
of Albion, New York. All the receivers
have flown off their cradles and hover
like tiny black angels. A single voice
that she can't recognize is calling her:
her mother or dead daughter, the hollow
voice of God. The tiny aluminum mouths
of the coin returns are spitting quarter

after quarter after quarter, more silver
than she'd need to buy eternity. Streets
are deserted and, invisible in its bright
red freshly painted scaffold, the lost
fire bell clangs and clangs its last alarm.

Fireflies

The sweet smell of wild straw-
berries and hay crushed in my
back, thirty years ago I'd fall
asleep with flashes of fireflies
by my bed, a whole tribe of eyes,
the guardian angels of my genes.

Now it's winter where I live
and each breath I take is rye.
Curled up in my percale pasture,
a foetus praying the terrible
dark for sleep, the lucifern
light of their deaths and lives
still blinks on and off inside
the glass of my balding head.

The glow of my grandmother's
gangrene. My godmother's cells
scorched whiter and whiter in her
memory. Cancer's blood-blue
ember in my father's throat.
I wait for that mysterious fuel
to exhaust itself, the almost
inaudible click of one worm's
corpse falling into final dark.

They won't burn out. They will
not die. They flash and flash,

a borealis in my clenched eyes.
They carve their shadows in this
glass growing thinner every night.
A spark's ignited at the center of
my skull. Soon we'll all be free.

Wildebeest in Sunlight

She comes to curl up in the patch
of sunlight on the white wool rug.

But with her instinct for the slow
solemnity of oriental royalty,

she arranges every limb until each
muscle is in place, each tendon

poised and orchestrated to hold court
in your living room or lie in state.

The sun regales her with attention;
soon each tip of fur radiates into

a borealis crown around the blank jade
of her eyes, and you blink hard just

to recall: This is a farmyard cat,
the litter's runt you rescued from

the burlap bag and brook. She sat
there in your bathroom every day

and looked on, mindless; she slept
on your bed like a mother or a life-

long lover; she begged you for her
food and, as you watched, squatted

shamelessly inside her litter-box.
Now she's too old to be anybody's

prisoner or pet, too ancient to obey
any other law except the last:

she's come to curl up on the patch
of sunlight by your feet to die.

While all regal tension escapes her
instinctively like a flock of birds,

while her muscles slacken into rigor
mortis, her eyes open to engulf your

life, her pupils dilate into total
absence, staring desperately; while

all the world she's known and all
the weight and measure of your days

sink in, at last, to the only glimpse
of wisdom she will ever know, her last

breath leaps and rises into sunlight,
suddenly ignites, wraps you in its

fur of fire, purrs into your soul
the peace of creatures without souls

and, with a gesture of ascension,
catapults into the center of its own

massive gravity where her life and
yours are one and free and cancelled out.

*

The Forest Lawn Community Mausoleum

is open for inspection. Come with me,
we'll visit those little rooms where
we can live forever, pick one out
ahead of time, one for each of us.

While we're there, we might as well
visit the crematory chapel, too,
inspect the services those ovens
offer. We might decide to rise

like bread, flare into martyrs
whose blood is fuel or quenches
the flame, choose to burn just
one more time, but with a last

amazing passion our bodies never
could have known before our souls
fly up the chimney and evaporate
in sky. Maybe we can buy urns.

We could put the ashes of burnt
pictures of ourselves in them
placed on our mantel and get used
to those little round eternal beds,

their intricate canopies guaranteed
to seal us in airtight. If we
choose very carefully, we could even
give ourselves away as presents

to close friends after we died.
They'd hear the perpetual stirring
of ashes and know the way the dead
live. At any rate, we'd use up less

space in the community mausoleum
and maybe be among more friends.
Imagine how lonely it must be to
be buried, separated from every-

body by coffins, false caskets, yards
and yards of loam muffling the motion
and voices of loved ones who come
to pay their respect. Imagine the long,

long loneliness of Tutankhamen
at the very center of that huge
chamber in the middle of the desert,
or of the Unknown Soldier, guarded

day and night, precision's prisoner
without rights. But now that
The Forest Lawn Community Mausoleum
is open for inspection, oh all

my neighbors, brothers, lovers,
come with me: if we must be
dead forever, then it's far, far
better to be dead all together.

*

Two Harvests

I

Huge bulging vans haul vegetables
and fruit to the deep-freeze factory.

At night the heads of cabbages hum,
their green blank faces perfectly
content, waiting to be born again

any time during the coming year,
waiting for warmth, for eyes
and noses, waiting for mouths.

2

All week truck-loads of apples
and squash ground and ground
their way up to the deep-freeze.

From inside that unrelenting dark,
at night we can hear the blank mouths
of anonymous produce wail in unison:

These are the fruits of your labor:
Heads of fathers and lovers, dead.

*

Omens, Prayers & Songs

POEMS AFTER THE CATAWBA

if you repeat these tales
in the summer or the dark
a snake will be waiting
waiting to bite your tongue

BIRDS

birds are singing around my door
they're talking and singing
someone's coming someone's coming

BURNING SASSAFRAS

I am burning grapevines
I am burning sassafras
the moon is swallowing the smoke

I'll tell lies all summer
all the women will believe me

RIVER SNAKE

my branch my son
don't go in the river

the snake in that water
is bigger than your mother

it'll wrap itself around you
and you'll never come back
you'll never never come back

LUCK-DREAMS

sometimes I dream of snakes
I know I won't be lucky
sometimes I dream of money
I know I will be lucky

what did you dream last night
was your dream good last night

last night I dreamt of nothing

SALAMANDER

I heard a salamander
barking in the dark

I am going to die

PRAYER TO THE TURTLE

I am eating your heart
I am eating your ancient heart
I will live a long time
I will live a very long time
I will die very very hard

MELON PATCH

the land was good
I planted a melon patch
I drove sticks all around it
someone came to steal my melons
all my sticks turned into snakes

HUNGRY BIRDS

it was cold last night
and it snowed
the birds were hungry

today the sun is out
the rocks are warm
the birds are glad
they're singing in their nests

we'll make traps
catch the birds
we'll have something to eat

POSSUM HUNTING

tonight we'll go hunting possum
we'll catch one and we'll eat it
bring a good dog and an axe
blow your horn cut down the tree

the possum climbed a big oak tree
it climbed a big and white oak tree
and I can't cut it down

SONG OF THE SICK

I'm sick I'm very sick
put me to bed give me medicine
now all stand around me
stand around me and be happy
sing and dance around me
I'm already feeling better

DANCING GHOSTS

the sun has set it's dark
my father and mother
stand by the open door

across the river
where an ancient village
used to be someone's drumming
someone's drumming hard
people are singing and dancing

but no one's there
no one's been there for years
there is no one there

WIDOW'S TABOO

your husband's dead
no one will talk to you
for one year your tongue
will be in his mouth

*

Migrating Season

Transfigured by excitement, they are
transparent as hair nets, hair white air.
They don't say a word, but as we ride
by the penitentiary, each of these two
aged sisters raises one small fragile fist:
light glows in the blue-veined milk of wrists.

Then all the way to Buffalo they just
sit in the front of the Greyhound bus,
their paper hands down on their laps.
They stare at the still migrating flocks
in late fall's sky and wish they were geese.

Geese

IN MEMORY OF ADA AND ARCHIBALD MACLEISH

The scalene angle's point pierces the horizon;
light tears. The V widens for miles. Another.
Then another. The sky darkens, the air throbs
under the pound of wings, cracks to the call
of hundreds of them migrating back to Canada.
After a multi-thousand-mile flight over oceans
and mountains and jungles and cities, and, almost
home, these geese soar over the last Great Lake,
as sure of their target as missiles or angels
deployed by gods. Unarmed by the awe that fills
our open mouths season after season, all we can
do is stare.
             We are the unbelievers who have
trod the moon's white dust in disbelief and jet-
tisoned magnetic waves of our voice, the radar
of our heart toward uncharted galaxies to trace
even just one other planet's pulse and prove that
in this cosmos we are not unique—only to return
to earth, the terminus of our trajectory, more
human, more alone.
                   Now in the soft tilled loam
of our friend's family garden, as we track today's
last flock of northbound geese, almost invisible
against the darkened sky, we are rooted in a moment
of amazement under arcs of brilliant single sylla-
bles of breath, ignited in our throats and blooming
in the early evening air like exploding rockets
at a local county fair celebrating still another
season's harvest.
                  Our faces, our hands are
raised by a supplication that starts in our feet
and clings to the lip of the last wing-feather

as it suddenly bursts into flame with sunlight
and starlight and, a dazzling pentecostal
tongue, plunges deep into the opposite horizon.
Stunned, our arms wrapped around each other in
a warmth of friendship, frost of fear, we walk
back into the house that hovers gently in the dark,
a familiar, ancient ship.

And when we speak again,
softly, anxious as first lovers or as lovers who
have lived a lifetime when they go to bed, we will
not speak of another season's longing or of one
more and more inexorable migration, but we shall
speak about the garden to be sown, the brilliance
of the stars, this gift that makes our bodies ache.

*

Moon-Rocks

National Air & Space Museum
Washington, D.C.

What else did we expect they'd find, those first
two astronauts who landed
on the moon, reduced to less than human
scale by the dimension of
the moment that unfolded right before
our eyes huddled by the moon-
glow of television sets in darkened
living rooms? The artifacts
of planetary angels who became
extinct at the moment breath
was first breathed into human blood? Ruins
of another lost world,
Atlantis risen from Pacific tides?
No more, perhaps, than just half
of one crudely chiseled arrowhead?

We already knew the moon
never could sustain life as we know it.
While Mike Collins sailed the lunar
orbit of the mother-craft alone,
Neil Armstrong and Buzz Aldrin
did precisely what they had
been trained to do: walk across the barren
landscape of our dreams, more slowly than we
had remembered, and gather
rocks no bigger than our fists and hearts
shaped by galactic winds.

Locked in a man-made bezel of far
more common substance, each day

now they're on display for old
witnesses and adolescent skeptics
to come see for themselves and,
trembling with regret or scorn, dare to touch
one more small, pale moon-rock worn
smooth by the kiss of a million other
swirled fingertips of pilgrims.

Fall Light

My tumbler of pale
apple juice this Sunday
afternoon, before
time falls back into
that quicker harvest
of the dark, picks up
orbs of late October
light from the burnished
and waxed table top,
distilling them into
that more aromatic hue
of Old Mr. Boston's
apricot brandy
we sipped on such days
on the Atlantic coast
before you stood in that
gold flood, that rampage
of maples at high noon,
flung your half-eaten
apple from your mouth,
leapt the cemetery gate
and, like a famished doe,
the pit of your eyes glazed,
fled and vanished, simply
fled and vanished back into
the evergreen wilderness
of our New England past.

Cartesian Char Woman

She cleans our quarters only once
a week, but, bristling

with old fashion mops and brooms,
she arrives as resolute

as a classic syllogism,
complete with inherent

human flaws: 1) a place where people
live and work, well, ought

to be clean; 2) that's what I'm paid to do;
3) therefore, I clean.

The odor of her logic is
more convincing than

Kandinsky's triangle: ammonia,
Ajax, Easy-Off,

lemon for our more expensive wood.
As wall-eyed as

a French philosopher, she starts
to work. No speck or spot

escapes: while her left eye's focused
on a coffee stain

in our rug, her right eye's roaming
all around the room

in search of dust and fingerprints,
the rubble of our

all too chaotic lives. Without
a word, this woman

sees the flaw in our hard work at
our sullen craft

and art, at making names for our
selves. Her life is one

simple formula of thesis,
antithesis, syn-

thesis. And when her work is done,
she sleeps more deeply

than we ever will in her solid
reconciliation with

her fate in our dirty world:
I am, therefore I clean.

*

Flute Making

Cleave it, then,
trim off the leafy end,
those tough and bitter greens.
Wash it off and boil it
till the meat is bleached.

Take that clean bone
to the trembling desert
of the highest rooftop
and set it out to dry.

Keep watch over it.
Sit cross-legged and serene
in your most perfect lotus
moving with the sun and moon.
Let no shadow dampen it.
Beware of birds.

Let the sun dry out
the marrow. Lift the bone
up to your lips, gently
suck the powder,
and with your breath's
open hand scatter its dry seeds.

Let the bone dry still,
still more. Let it dry until
it glows, until your eyes
are burning jets of fever.

And when the sun
and moon are burning

in the same blue eye,
when seeds clatter
in your hip,
when your tongue
is bone, when the bone
is pure and dry,

then hone one end
until it's smooth
against your lips,
until your tongue
is comfortable on it.

Carve out the stops,
absolutely round.
Decorate it:
exquisite scrimshaw
from a perfect tusk.

Now play it.
Make music.
High, pure notes,
inhuman octaves.

Love, play
that fine flute
of my right arm.

*

Totem

Year in, year out, I've shed my skin
and hair, my teeth and sperm,
perfect invisible antlers. Animal,
I've moulted friends and names.

Bones of strangers blow like bugles.
Hands ring. Tongues roll. A mob
of admiration starts to break and crush.

My ghosts roam the streets and wail.
I am arriving to myself.

*

Aubade

This morning
a thin rain
pierced my soft
belly's skin &
probed for roots.

Falling back
to sleep, I was
an empty field
with just one
cedar rising
from my center,
erect, a marvel-
ous temple.

Rain scratched
my window pane:
silver claws
of sheer, flesh-
less angels. I
woke to sunlight.

Small bright green
beasts blossomed on
my shining bones'
enameled limbs,
shed petals of
pure song in
morning air &
beat down psalms.

*

Easter Sunday

All moisture's been sucked out of me.
I've turned in and on myself. Layers
of stale pastry, my skin flakes: Buddha
crumbling at last and falling into place.

In the basket of my dust, my friends
will find what was twisted in me,
always grating on my ribs: a thin
and indestructible scroll, undecipher-

able ancient characters I could never
understand: *You will live forever.*

*

Cave Dwellers

I've carved a cave in the mountainside.
I've drilled for water, stocked provisions
to last a lifetime. The walls are smooth.
We can live here, love, safe from elements.
We'll invent another love that can't destroy.
We'll make exquisite reproductions of our
selves, immortal on these walls.

                And when
this sea that can't support us is burned clean,
when the first new creatures crawl from it,
gasping for water, air, more wondrous and more
wild than earth's first couple, they shall see
there were two before them: you and me.

*

A. Poulin, Jr. was born in Lisbon, Maine, in 1938 of French-Canadian immigrants, Alfred Poulin and Alice Michaud. He received a B.A. from St. Francis College (Maine), an M.A. from Loyola University (Chicago), and an M.F.A. from the University of Iowa. He has taught at each of the colleges and universities from which he received degrees, as well as for the University of Maryland (European Division, Germany), the University of New Hampshire, and the State University of New York, College at Brockport. He also has been Visiting Fulbright Lecturer in Contemporary American Poetry at the Universities of Athens and Thessaloniki, Greece.

The recipient of fellowships from The National Endowment for the Arts for both Poetry and Translation, Poulin also has received grants and fellowships from The Research Foundation of the State University of New York, The Translation Center of Columbia University, The New York Foundation for the Arts, and the Embassy of Canada. In 1989 He also was awarded an honorary Doctor of Humane Letters degree by the University of New England.

A. Poulin, Jr. is founding editor and publisher of BOA Editions, Ltd. He resides in Brockport, New York, with his wife, the metalsmith and jeweler, Basilike Poulin.

*

The text and cover of this book were designed by Tree Swenson.

The Galliard type was designed by Matthew Carter and set by The Typeworks.

Manufactured by Thomson-Shore.